MEMORY AND RECONCILIATION: THE CHURCH AND THE FAULTS OF THE PAST

and

Homily of John Paul II

Mass for the Day of Pardon

International Theological Commission

MEMORY AND RECONCILIATION: THE CHURCH AND THE FAULTS OF THE PAST

December, 1999

and

Homily of John Paul II

Mass for the Day of Pardon

March 12, 2000

BOOKS & MEDIA
BOSTON

ISBN 0-8198-4809-3

Vatican Translation

Printed and published in the U.S.A. by Pauline Books & Media, 50 Saint Pauls Avenue, Boston MA 02130-3491.

www.pauline.org

Pauline Books & Media is the publishing house of the Daughters of St. Paul, an international congregation of women religious serving the Church with the communications media.

1 2 3 4 5 6 7 05 04 03 02 01 00

Contents

Preliminary Note

The study of the topic "The Church and the Faults of the Past" was proposed to the International Theological Commission by its President, Joseph Cardinal Ratzinger, in view of the celebration of the Jubilee Year 2000. A subcommission was established to prepare this study; it was composed of Rev. Christopher Begg, Msgr. Bruno Forte (President), Rev. Sebastian Karotemprel, S.D.B., Msgr. Roland Minnerath, Rev. Thomas Norris, Rev. Rafael Salazar Cardenas, M.Sp.S., and Msgr. Anton Strukelj. The general discussion of this theme took place in numerous meetings of the subcommission and during the plenary sessions of the International Theological Commission held in Rome from 1998 to 1999. By written vote, the present text was approved in *forma specifica* by the Commission, and was then submitted to the President, Cardinal Ratzinger, Prefect of the Congregation for the Doctrine of the Faith, who gave his approval for its publication.

Introduction

The Bull of Indiction of the Great Jubilee of the Year 2000, *Incarnationis Mysterium* (November 29, 1998), includes the purification of memory among the signs "which may help people to live the exceptional grace of the Jubilee with greater fervor." This purification aims at liberating personal and communal conscience from all forms of resentment and violence that are the legacy of past faults, through a renewed historical and theological evaluation of such events. This should lead—if done correctly—to a corresponding recognition of guilt and contribute to the path of reconciliation. Such a process can have a significant effect on the present, precisely because the consequences of past faults still make themselves felt and can persist as tensions in the present.

The purification of memory is thus "an act of courage and humility in recognizing the wrongs done by those who have borne or bear the name of Christian." It is based on the conviction that because of "the bond which unites us to one another in the Mystical Body, all of us, though not personally responsible and without encroaching on the judgment of God, who alone knows every heart, bear the burden of the errors and faults of those who have gone before us." John Paul II adds: "As the successor of Peter, I ask that in this year of mercy the Church, strong in the holiness which she receives from her Lord, should kneel before God and implore forgiveness for the past and present sins of her sons and daughters."[1] In reiterating that "Christians are invited to acknowledge, before God and before those offended by their actions, the faults which they have committed," the Pope concludes, "Let them do so without seeking anything in return, but strengthened only by 'the love of God which has been poured into our hearts' (Rom 5:5)."[2]

The requests for forgiveness made by the Bishop of Rome in this spirit of authenticity and gratuitousness have given rise to various reactions. The unconditional trust in the power of truth which the Pope has shown has met with a generally favorable reception both inside and outside the Church. Many have noted the increased credibility of ecclesial pronouncements that has resulted from this way of acting. Some reservations, however, have also been voiced, mainly expressions of unease connected with particular historical and cultural contexts in which the simple admission of faults committed by the sons and daughters of the Church may look like acquiescence in the face of accusations made by those who are prejudicially hostile to the Church. Between agreement and unease, the need

---

1. *Incarnationis Mysterium,* 11.

2. *Ibid.* In numerous prior statements, in particular, number 33 of the Apostolic Letter *Tertio Millennio Adveniente,* the Pope has indicated to the Church the path forward for purifying her memory regarding the faults of the past and for giving an example of repentance to individuals and civil societies.

arises for a reflection which clarifies the reasons, the conditions, and the exact form of the requests for forgiveness for the faults of the past.

The International Theological Commission, in which a diversity of cultures and sensitivities within the one Catholic faith are represented, decided to address this need with the present text. The text offers a theological reflection on the conditions which make acts of "purification of memory" possible in connection with the recognition of the faults of the past. The questions it seeks to address are as follows: Why should it be done? Who should do it? What is the goal and how should this be determined, by correctly combining historical and theological judgment? Who will be addressed? What are the moral implications? And what are the possible effects on the life of the Church and on society? The purpose of the text is, therefore, not to examine particular historical cases but rather to clarify the presuppositions that ground repentance for past faults.

Having noted the kind of reflection which will be presented here, it is important also to make clear what is referred to when the text speaks of the Church: it is not a question of the historical institution alone or solely the spiritual communion of those whose hearts are illumined by faith. The Church is understood as the community of the baptized, inseparably visible and operating in history under the direction of her pastors, united as a profound mystery by the action of the life-giving Spirit. According to the Second Vatican Council, the Church "by a strong analogy is compared to the mystery of the incarnate Word. In fact, as the assumed nature is at the service of the divine Word as a living instrument of salvation, indissolubly united to him, so also in a not dissimilar way, the social structure of the

Church is at the service of the Spirit of Christ which vivifies it for the building up of the body" (cf. Eph 4:16).[3]

This Church, which embraces her sons and daughters of the past and of the present, in a real and profound communion, is the sole mother of grace who takes upon herself also the weight of past faults in order to purify memory and to live the renewal of heart and life according to the will of the Lord. She is able to do this insofar as Christ Jesus, whose Mystical Body extended through history she is, has taken upon himself once and for all the sins of the world.

The structure of the text mirrors the questions posed. It moves from a brief historical revisiting of the theme (Chapter 1), in order to be able to investigate the biblical foundation (Chapter 2) and explore more deeply the theological conditions of the requests for forgiveness (Chapter 3). The precise correlation of historical and theological judgment is a decisive element for reaching correct and efficacious statements that take proper account of the times, places and contexts in which the actions under consideration were situated (Chapter 4). The final considerations, that have a specific value for the Catholic Church, are dedicated to the moral (Chapter 5), pastoral and missionary (Chapter 6) implications of these acts of repentance for the faults of the past. Nevertheless, in the knowledge that the necessity of recognizing one's own faults has reason to be practiced by all peoples and religions, one hopes that the proposed reflections may help everyone to advance on the path of truth, fraternal dialogue, and reconciliation.

---

3. *Lumen Gentium,* 8.

At the conclusion of this introduction, it may be useful to recall the purpose of every act of "purification of memory" undertaken by believers, because this is what has inspired the work of the Commission: it is the glorification of God, because living in obedience to divine truth and its demands leads to confessing, together with our faults, the eternal mercy and justice of the Lord. The *"confessio peccati,"* sustained and illuminated by faith in the truth which frees and saves *("confessio fidei"),* becomes a *"confessio laudis"* addressed to God, before whom alone it becomes possible to recognize the faults both of the past and of the present, so that we might be reconciled by and to him in Christ Jesus, the only Savior of the world, and become able to forgive those who have offended us. This offer of forgiveness appears particularly meaningful when one thinks of the many persecutions suffered by Christians in the course of history. In this perspective, the actions undertaken by the Holy Father, and those requested by him, regarding the faults of the past have an exemplary and prophetic value, for religions as much as for governments and nations, beyond being of value for the Catholic Church, which is thus helped to live in a more efficacious way the Great Jubilee of the Incarnation as an event of grace and reconciliation for everyone.

1. The Problem: Yesterday and Today

1.1. Before Vatican II

The Jubilee has always been lived in the Church as a time of joy for the salvation given in Christ and as a privileged occasion for penance and reconciliation for the sins present in the lives of the People of God. From its first celebration under Boniface VIII in 1300, the penitential pilgrimage to the tombs of the Apostles Peter and Paul was associated with the granting of an exceptional indulgence for procuring, with sacramental pardon, total or partial remission of the temporal punishment due to sin.[4] In this context, both sacramental forgiveness and the remission of temporal punishment have a personal character. In the course of the "year of pardon and grace,"[5] the Church dispenses in a particular way the treasury of grace that Christ

4. Cf. *Extravagantes Communes,* lib. V, tit. IX, c. 1 (A. Friedberg, *Corpus Iuris Canonici,* t. II, c. 1304).

5. Cf. Benedict XIV, Letter *Salutis Nostrae,* April 30, 1774, § 2. Leo XII in the Letter *Quod hoc Ineunte,* May 24, 1824, §2 speaks of the "year of expiation, forgiveness and redemption, of grace, remission and of indulgence."

has constituted for her benefit.[6] In none of the Jubilees celebrated till now has there been, however, an awareness in conscience of any faults in the Church's past, nor of the need to ask God's pardon for conduct in the recent or remote past.

Indeed, in the entire history of the Church there are no precedents for requests for forgiveness by the Magisterium for past wrongs. Councils and papal decrees applied sanctions, to be sure, to abuses of which clerics and laymen were found guilty, and many pastors sincerely strove to correct them. However, the occasions when ecclesiastical authorities—Pope, bishops, or councils—have openly acknowledged the faults or abuses which they themselves were guilty of, have been quite rare. One famous example is furnished by the reforming Pope Adrian VI who acknowledged publicly in a message to the Diet of Nuremberg of November 25, 1522, "the abominations, the abuses...and the lies" of which the "Roman court" of his time was guilty, "deep-rooted and extensive...sickness," extending "from the top to the members."[7] Adrian VI deplored the faults of his times, precisely those of his immediate predecessor Leo X and his curia, without, however, adding a request for pardon.

---

6. This is the sense of the definition of indulgence given by Clement VI when in 1343 he instituted the practice of having a Jubilee every fifty years. Clement VI sees in the Church's Jubilee "the spiritual accomplishment" of the "Jubilee of remission and of joy" in the Old Testament (Lv 25).

7. "Each of us must examine [his conscience] with respect to what he has fallen into and examine himself even more rigorously than God will on the day of his wrath" in *Deutsche Reichstagsakten,* new series, III, 390–399 (Gotha, 1893).

It will be necessary to wait until Paul VI to find a Pope express a request for pardon addressed as much to God as to a group of contemporaries. In his address at the opening of the second session of the Second Vatican Council, the Pope asked "pardon of God...and of the separated brethren" of the East who may have felt offended "by us" (the Catholic Church), and declared himself ready for his part to pardon offenses received. In the view of Paul VI, both the request for and offer of pardon concerned solely the sin of the division between Christians and presupposed reciprocity.

1.2. The Teaching of the Council

Vatican II takes the same approach as Paul VI. For the faults committed against unity, the Council Fathers state, "we ask pardon of God and of the separated brethren, as we forgive those who trespass against us."[8] In addition to faults against unity, it noted other negative episodes from the past for which Christians bore some responsibility. Thus, "it deplores certain attitudes that sometimes are found among Christians" and which led people to think that faith and science are mutually opposed.[9] Likewise, it considers the fact that in "the genesis of atheism," Christians may have had "some responsibility" insofar as through their negligence they "conceal rather than reveal the authentic face of God and religion."[10] In addition, the Council "deplores" the persecu-

8. *Unitatis Redintegratio,* 7.

9. *Gaudium et Spes,* 36.

10. *Ibid.,* 19.

tions and manifestations of anti-Semitism "in every time and on whoever's part."[11] The Council, nevertheless, does not add a request for pardon for the things cited.

From a theological point of view, Vatican II distinguishes between the indefectible fidelity of the Church and the weaknesses of her members, clergy or laity, yesterday and today,[12] and therefore, between the Bride of Christ "with neither blemish nor wrinkle...holy and immaculate" (cf. Eph 5:27), and her children, pardoned sinners, called to permanent *metanoia,* to renewal in the Holy Spirit. "The Church, embracing sinners in her bosom, is at the same time holy and always in need of purification, and incessantly pursues the path of penance and renewal."[13]

The Council also elaborated some criteria of discernment regarding the guilt or responsibility of persons now living for faults of the past. In effect, the Council recalled in two different contexts the non-imputability to those now living of past faults committed by members of their religious communities:

- "What was committed during the passion (of Christ) cannot be imputed either indiscriminately to all Jews then living nor to the Jews of our time."[14]

---

11. *Nostra Aetate,* 4.

12. *Gaudium et Spes,* 43 §6.

13. *Lumen Gentium,* 8; cf. *Unitatis Redintegratio,* 6: "Christ summons the Church, as she goes her pilgrim way, to that continual reform of which she always has need, insofar as she is a human institution here on earth."

14. *Nostra Aetate,* 4.

• "Large communities became separated from full communion with the Catholic Church—at times not without the fault of men on both sides. However, one cannot charge with the sin of separation those who now are born into these communities and who in these are instructed in the faith of Christ, and the Catholic Church embraces them with fraternal respect and love."[15]

When the first Holy Year was celebrated after the Council, in 1975, Paul VI gave it the theme of "renewal and reconciliation,"[16] making clear in the Apostolic Exhortation *Paterna cum Benevolentia* that reconciliation should take place first of all among the faithful of the Catholic Church.[17] As in its origin, the Holy Year remained an occasion for conversion and reconciliation of sinners to God by means of the sacramental economy of the Church.

1.3. John Paul II's Requests for Forgiveness

Not only did John Paul II renew expressions of regret for the "sorrowful memories" that mark the history of the divisions among Christians, as Paul VI and the Second Vatican Council had done,[18] but he also extended a request for forgiveness to a

---

15. *Unitatis Redintegratio,* 3.

16. Cf. Paul VI, Apostolic Letter *Apostolorum Limina,* May 23, 1974 (*Enchiridion Vaticanum* 5, 305).

17. Paul VI, Exhortation *Paterna cum Benevolentia,* December 8, 1974 (*Enchiridion Vaticanum* 5, 526–553).

18. Cf. Encyclical Letter *Ut Unum Sint,* May 25, 1995, 88: "To the extent that we are responsible for these, I join my predecessor Paul VI in asking forgiveness."

multitude of historical events in which the Church, or individual groups of Christians, were implicated in different respects.[19] In the Apostolic Letter *Tertio Millennio Adveniente,*[20] the Pope expresses the hope that the Jubilee of 2000 might be the occasion for a purification of the memory of the Church from all forms of "counterwitness and scandal" which have occurred in the course of the past millennium.[21]

The Church is invited to "become more fully conscious of the sinfulness of her children." She "acknowledges as her own her sinful sons and daughters" and encourages them "to purify themselves, through repentance, of past errors and instances of infidelity, inconsistency and slowness to act."[22] The responsibility of Christians for the evils of our time is likewise noted,[23] although the accent falls particularly on the solidarity of the Church of today with past faults. Some of these are explicitly

---

19. For example, the Pope, addressing himself to the Moravians, asked "forgiveness, on behalf of all Catholics, for the wrongs caused to non-Catholics in the course of history" (cf. Canonization of Jan Sarkander in the Czech Republic, May 21, 1995). The Holy Father also wanted to undertake "an act of expiation" and ask forgiveness of the Indians of Latin America and from the Africans deported as slaves (*Message to the Indians of America,* Santo Domingo, October 13, 1992, and *General Audience Discourse* of October 21, 1992). Ten years earlier he had already asked forgiveness from the Africans for the way in which they had been treated (*Discourse* at Yaoundé, August 13, 1985).

20. Cf. *Tertio Millennio Adveniente,* 33–36.

21. Cf. *ibid.,* 33.

22. *Ibid.,* 33.

23. Cf. *ibid.,* 36.

mentioned, like the separation of Christians,[24] or the "methods of violence and intolerance" used in the past to evangelize.[25]

John Paul II also promoted the deeper theological exploration of the idea of taking responsibility for the wrongs of the past and of possibly asking forgiveness from one's contemporaries,[26] when in the Exhortation *Reconciliatio et Paenitentia,* he states that in the sacrament of Penance "the sinner stands alone before God with his sin, repentance, and trust. No one can repent in his place or ask forgiveness in his name." Sin is therefore always personal, even though it wounds the entire Church, which, represented by the priest as minister of Penance, is the sacramental mediatrix of the grace which reconciles with God.[27] Also the situations of "social sin"—which are evident in the human community when justice, freedom and peace are damaged—are always "the result of the accumulation and concentration of many personal sins." While moral responsibility may become diluted in anonymous causes, one can only speak of social sin by way of analogy.[28] It emerges from this that the imputability of a fault cannot properly be extended beyond the group of persons who had consented to it voluntarily, by means of acts or omissions, or through negligence.

---

24. Cf. *ibid.,* 34.

25. Cf. *ibid.,* 35.

26. This final aspect appears in *Tertio Millennio Adveniente* only in number 33, where it is said that the Church "before God and man" acknowledges as her own her sinful sons and daughters.

27. John Paul II, Exhortation *Reconciliatio et Paenitentia,* December 2, 1984, 31.

28. *Ibid.,* 16.

1.4. The Questions Raised

The Church is a living society spanning the centuries. Her memory is not constituted only by the tradition which goes back to the apostles and is normative for her faith and life, but she is also rich in the variety of historical experiences, positive and negative, which she has lived. In large part, the Church's past structures her present. The doctrinal, liturgical, canonical and ascetical tradition nourishes the life of the believing community, offering it an incomparable sampling of models to imitate.

Along the entire earthly pilgrimage, however, the good grain always remains inextricably mixed with the chaff; holiness stands side by side with infidelity and sin.[29] And it is thus that the remembrance of scandals of the past can become an obstacle to the Church's witness today, and the recognition of the past faults of the Church's sons and daughters of yesterday can foster renewal and reconciliation in the present.

The difficulty that emerges is that of defining past faults, above all, because of the historical judgment which this requires. In events of the past, one must always distinguish the responsibility or fault that can be attributed to members of the Church as believers from that which should be referred to society during the centuries of 'Christendom' or to power structures in which the temporal and spiritual were closely intertwined. An historical hermeneutic is therefore more necessary

29. Cf. Mt 13:24–30; 36–43; St. Augustine, *De Civitate Dei,* I, 35: *CCL* 47, 33; XI, 1: *CCL* 48, 321; XIX, 26: *CCL* 48, 696.

than ever in order to distinguish correctly between the action of the Church as community of faith and that of society in the times when an osmosis existed between them.

The steps taken by John Paul II to ask pardon for faults of the past have been understood in many circles as signs of the Church's vitality and authenticity, such that they strengthen her credibility. It is right, moreover, that the Church contribute to changing false and unacceptable images of herself, especially in those areas in which, whether through ignorance or bad faith, some sectors of opinion like to identify her with obscurantism and intolerance. The requests for pardon formulated by the Pope have also given rise to positive emulation both inside and outside the Church. Heads of state or government, private and public associations, religious communities are today asking forgiveness for episodes or historical periods marked by injustices. This practice is far from just an exercise in rhetoric, and for this reason, some hesitate to do so, calculating the attendant costs—among which are those on the legal plane—of an acknowledgment of past wrongs. Also from this point of view, a rigorous discernment is necessary.

Nevertheless, some of the faithful are disconcerted and their loyalty to the Church seems shaken. Some wonder how they can hand on a love for the Church to younger generations if this same Church is imputed with crimes and faults. Others observe that the recognition of faults is for the most part one-sided and is exploited by the Church's detractors, who are satisfied to see the Church confirm the prejudices they had of her. Still others warn against arbitrarily making current generations of believers feel guilty for shortcomings they did not consent to in any way, even though they declare themselves ready to take responsibility to the extent that some groups of people still feel themselves affected today by the consequences of injustices suffered by their forebears in previous times.

Others hold that the Church could purify her memory with respect to ambiguous actions in which she was involved in the past simply by taking part in the critical work on memory developed in our society. Thus she could affirm that she joins with her contemporaries in rejecting what the moral conscience of our time reproaches, though without putting herself forward as the only guilty party responsible for the evils of the past, by seeking at the same time a dialogue in mutual understanding with those who may feel themselves still wounded by past acts imputable to the children of the Church.

Finally, it is to be expected that certain groups might demand that forgiveness be sought in their regard, either by analogy with other groups, or because they believe that they have suffered wrongs. In any case, the purification of memory can never mean that the Church ceases to proclaim the revealed truth that has been entrusted to her whether in the area of faith or of morals.

Thus, a number of questions can be identified: Can today's conscience be assigned "guilt" for isolated historical phenomena like the Crusades or the Inquisition? Isn't it a bit too easy to judge people of the past by the conscience of today (as the Scribes and Pharisees do according to Mt 23:29–32), almost as if moral conscience were not situated in time? And, on the other hand, can it be denied that ethical judgment is always possible, given the simple fact that the truth of God and its moral requirements always have value?

Whatever attitude is adopted must come to terms with these questions and seek answers that are based in revelation and in its living transmission in the faith of the Church. The first question is therefore that of clarifying the extent to which requests for forgiveness for past wrongs, especially if addressed to groups of people today, are within the biblical and theological horizon of reconciliation with God and neighbor.

2. Biblical Approach

The investigation of Israel's acknowledgment of faults in the Old Testament and the topic of the confession of faults as found in the traditions of the New Testament can be developed in various ways.[30] The theological nature of the reflection undertaken here leads us to favor a largely thematic approach, centering on the following question: What background does the testimony of Sacred Scripture furnish for John Paul II's invitation to the Church to confess the faults of the past?

2.1. The Old Testament

Confessions of sins and corresponding requests for forgiveness can be found throughout the Bible—in the narratives of the Old Testament, in the psalms, and in the prophets, as well as in the gospels of the New Testament. There are also sporadic references in the wisdom literature and in the letters of the New Testament. Given the abundance and diffusion of

---

30. On different methods of reading Sacred Scripture, see *The Interpretation of the Bible in the Church,* Pontifical Biblical Commission (1993).

these testimonies, the question arises of how to select and catalogue the mass of significant texts.

One may inquire here about the biblical texts related to the confession of sins: Who is confessing what (and what kind of fault) to whom? Put in this way, the question helps distinguish two principal categories of "confession texts," each of which embraces different subcategories, namely, a) confession texts of individual sins, and b) confession texts of sins of the entire people (and of those of their forebears). In relation to the recent ecclesial practice that motivates this study, we will restrict our analysis to the second category.

In this second category, different expressions can be found, depending on who is making the confession of the sins of the people and on who is, or is not, associated with the shared guilt, prescinding from the presence or absence of an awareness of personal responsibility (which has only matured progressively: cf. Ez 14:12–23; 18:1–32; 33:10–20). On the basis of these criteria, the following rather fluid cases can be distinguished:

- A first series of texts represents the entire people (sometimes personified as a single "I") who, in a particular moment of its history, confesses or alludes to its sins against God without any (explicit) reference to the faults of the preceding generations.[31]

31. In this series, for example, are: Dt 1:41 (the generation of the desert recognizes that it had sinned by refusing to go forward into the Promised Land); Jgs 10:10, 12 (in the time of the Judges the people twice say "we have sinned" against the Lord, referring to their service of the Baals); 1 Sm 7:6 (the people of Samuel's time say "we have sinned against the Lord!"); Nm 21:7 (this text is distinctive in that here the people of the generation of Moses admit that, in complaining about the

- Another group of texts places the confession—directed to God—of the current sins of the people on the lips of one or more leaders (religious), who may or may not include themselves explicitly among the sinful people for whom they are praying.[32]

- A third group of texts presents the people or one of their leaders in the act of mentioning the sins of their forebears without, however, making mention of those of the present generation.[33]

---

food, they had become guilty of "sin" because they had spoken against the Lord and against their human guide, Moses); 1 Sm 12:19 (the Israelites of the time of Samuel recognize that—by having asked for a king—they have added this to "all their sins"); Ezr 10:13 (the people acknowledge in front of Ezra that they had greatly "transgressed in this matter" [marrying foreign women]); Ps 65:2–3; 90:8; 103:10; (107:10–11, 17); Is 59:9–15; 64:5–9; Jer 8:14; 14:7; Lam 1:14, 18a, 22 (in which Jerusalem speaks in the first person); 3:42 (4:13); Bar 4:12–13 (Zion speaks of the sins of her children which led to her destruction); Ez 33:10; Mi 7:9 ("I"), 18–19.

32. For example: Ex 9:27 (Pharaoh says to Moses and Aaron: "This time I have sinned; the Lord is in the right; I and my people are guilty"); 34:9 (Moses prays "forgive our iniquity and our sin"); Lv 16:21 (the high priest confesses the sins of the people on the head of the "scapegoat" on the day of atonement); Ex 32:11–13 (cf. Dt 9:26–29: Moses); 32:31 (Moses); 1 Kgs 8:33 ff. (cf. 2 Chr 6:22 ff.: Solomon prays that God will forgive the future sins of the people); 2 Chr 28:13 (the leaders of the Israelites acknowledge "our guilt is already great"); Ezr 10:2 (Shecaniah says to Ezra "We have broken faith with our God, by marrying foreign women"); Neh 1:5–11 (Nehemiah confesses the sins committed by the people of Israel, by himself, and by the house of his father); Est 4:17(n) (Esther confesses: "We have sinned against you and you have delivered us into the hands of our enemies, because we have given glory to their gods"); 2 Mc 7:18–32 (the Jewish martyrs say that they are suffering because of "our sins" against God).

33. Among the examples of this type of national confession are: 2 Kgs 22:13 (cf. 2 Chr 34:21: Josiah fears the anger of the Lord "because

- More frequent are the confessions that mention the faults of the forebears, linking them expressly to the errors of the present generation.[34]

We can conclude from the testimonies gathered that in all cases where the "sins of the fathers" are mentioned, the confession is addressed solely to God, and the sins confessed by the people and for the people are those committed directly against him rather than those committed (also) against other human

---

our fathers did not heed the words of this book"); 2 Chr 29:6–7 (Hezekiah says "our fathers have been unfaithful"); Ps 78:8 ff. (the psalmist recounts the sins of past generations from the time of the exodus from Egypt). Cf. also the popular saying cited in Jer 31:29 and Ez 18:2: "The fathers have eaten sour grapes and the children's teeth are set on edge."

34. As in the following texts: Lv 26:40 (the exiles are called to "confess their iniquity and the iniquity of their fathers"); Ezr 9:5b–15 (the penitential prayer of Ezra, v. 7: "From the days of our fathers to this day we have been deeply guilty"; cf. Neh 9:6–37); Tb 3:1–5 (in his prayer Tobit prays: "Do not punish me for my sins and for my errors and those of my fathers" [v. 3] and continues with the statement: "We have not kept your commandments" [v. 5]; Ps 79:8–9 (this collective lament implores God: "Do not impute to us the offenses of our fathers...deliver us and forgive us our sins"); 106:6 ("Both we and our fathers have sinned"); Jer 3:25 ("...we have sinned against the Lord our God...we and our fathers"); Jer 14:19–22 ("We acknowledge our iniquity and the iniquity of our fathers," v. 20); Lam 5 ("Our fathers sinned and they are no more, and we bear the penalty for their iniquities" [v. 7]—"Woe to us for we have sinned" [v. 16b]; Bar 1:15—3:18 ("We have sinned against the Lord" [1:17, cf. 1:19, 21; 2:5, 24]—"Remember not the iniquities of our fathers" [3:5, cf. 2:33; 3:4, 7]); Dn 3:26–(the prayer of Azariah: "With truth and justice you have inflicted all this because of our sins": v. 28); Dn 9:4–19 ("On account of our sins and the iniquity of our fathers, Jerusalem [...has] become the reproach..." v. 16).

beings (only in Numbers 21:7 is mention made of a human party harmed, Moses).[35] The question arises as to why the biblical writers did not feel the need to address requests for forgiveness to present interlocutors for the sins committed by their fathers, given their strong sense of solidarity in good and evil among the generations (one thinks of the notion of "corporate personality").

We can propose various hypotheses in response to this question. First, there is the prevalent theocentrism of the Bible, which gives precedence to the acknowledgment, whether individual or national, of the faults committed against God. What is more, acts of violence perpetrated by Israel against other peoples, which would seem to require a request for forgiveness from those peoples or from their descendants, are understood to be the execution of divine directives, as for example Genesis 2–11 and Deuteronomy 7:2 (the extermination of the Canaanites), or 1 Samuel 15 and Deuteronomy 25:19 (the destruction of the Amalekites). In such cases, the involvement of a divine command would seem to exclude any possible request for forgiveness.[36] The experiences of maltreatment suffered by Israel at the hands of other peoples and the animosity thus aroused could also

35. These include failing to trust God (for example, Dt 1:41; Nm 14:10), idolatry (as in Jgs 10:10–15), requesting a human king (1 Sm 12:9), marrying foreign women contrary to the law of God (Ezr 9–10). In Isaiah 59:13b the people say of themselves that they are guilty of "talking oppression and revolt, conceiving lying words and uttering them from the heart."

36. Cf. the analogous case of the repudiation of foreign wives described in Ezra 9–10, with all the negative consequences which this would have had for these women. The question of a request for forgiveness addressed to them (and/or to their descendents) is not treated, since their repudiation is presented as a requirement of God's law (cf. Dt 7:3) in all these chapters.

have militated against the idea of asking pardon of these peoples for the evil done to them.[37]

In any case the sense of intergenerational solidarity in sin (and in grace) remains relevant in the biblical testimony and is expressed in the confession before God of the "sins of the fathers," such that John Paul II could state, citing the splendid prayer of Azariah:

"'Blessed are you, O Lord, the God of our fathers.... For we have sinned and transgressed by departing from you, and we have done every kind of evil. Your commandments we have not heeded or observed' (Dn 3:26, 29–30). This is how the Jews prayed after the exile (cf. also Bar 2:11–13), accepting the responsibility for the sins committed by their fathers. The Church imitates their example and also asks forgiveness for the historical sins of her children."[38]

2.2. The New Testament

A fundamental theme connected with the idea of guilt, and amply present in the New Testament, is that of the absolute holiness of God. The God of Jesus is the God of Israel (cf. Jn 4:22), invoked as "Holy Father" (Jn 17:11), and called "the

---

37. In this context, the case of the permanently strained relationship between Israel and Edom comes to mind. The Edomites as a people—despite the fact that they were Israel's "brother"—participated and rejoiced in the conquest of Jerusalem by the Babylonians (cf., for example, Ob 10–14). Israel, as a sign of outrage for this betrayal, felt no need to ask forgiveness for the killing of defenseless Edomite prisoners of war by King Amaziah as recounted in 2 Chronicles 25:12.

38. John Paul II, *General Audience Discourse* of September 1, 1999; in *L'Osservatore Romano,* Eng. ed., September 8, 1999, 7.

Holy One" in 1 John 2:20 (cf. Acts 6:10). The triple proclamation of God as "holy" in Isaiah 6:3 returns in Acts 4:8, while 1 Peter 1:16 insists on the fact that Christians must be holy "for it is written: 'You shall be holy, for I am holy'" (cf. Lv 11:44–45; 19:2).

All this reflects the Old Testament notion of the absolute holiness of God; however, for Christian faith the divine holiness has entered history in the person of Jesus of Nazareth. The Old Testament notion has not been abandoned but developed, in the sense that the holiness of God becomes present in the holiness of the incarnate Son (cf. Mk 1:24; Lk 1:35; 4:34; Jn 6:69; Acts 3:14; 4:27, 30; Rv 3:7), and the holiness of the Son is shared by "his own" (cf. Jn 17:16–19), who are made sons in the Son (cf. Gal 4:4–6; Rom 8:14–17). There can be no aspiration to divine sonship in Jesus unless there is love for one's neighbor (cf. Mk 12:29–31; Mt 22:37–38; Lk 10:27–28).

Love of neighbor, absolutely central in the teaching of Jesus, becomes the "new commandment" in the Gospel of John; the disciples should love as he has loved (cf. Jn 13:34–35; 15:12, 17), that is, perfectly, "to the end" (Jn 13:1). The Christian is called to love and to forgive to a degree that transcends every human standard of justice and produces a reciprocity between human beings, reflective of the reciprocity between Christ and the Father (cf. Jn 13:34 f.; 15:1–11; 17:21–26). In this perspective, great emphasis is given to the theme of reconciliation and forgiveness of faults.

Jesus asks his disciples to be always ready to forgive all those who have offended them, just as God himself always offers his forgiveness: "Forgive us our trespasses as we forgive those who trespass against us" (Mt 6:12; 6:12–15). He who is able to forgive his neighbor shows that he has understood his own need for forgiveness by God. The disciple is invited to forgive the one who offends him "seventy times seven," even if the person may not ask for forgiveness (cf. Mt 18:21–22).

With regard to someone who has been injured by another, Jesus insists that the injured person should take the first step, canceling the offense through forgiveness offered "from the heart" (cf. Mt 18:35; Mk 11:25), aware that he too is a sinner before God, who never refuses forgiveness sincerely entreated. In Matthew 5:23–24, Jesus asks the offender to "go and reconcile himself with his brother who has something against him" before presenting his offering at the altar. An act of worship on the part of one who has no desire beforehand to repair the damage to his neighbor is not pleasing to God. What matters is changing one's own heart and showing in an appropriate way that one really wants reconciliation.

The sinner, however, aware that his sins wound his relationship with God and with his neighbor (cf. Lk 15:21), can expect pardon only from God, because only God is always merciful and ready to cancel our sins. This is also the significance of the sacrifice of Christ who, once and for all, has purified us of our sins (cf. Heb 9:22; 10:18). Thus, the offender and the offended are reconciled by God who receives and forgives everyone in his mercy.

In this context, which could be expanded through an analysis of the Letters of Paul and the Catholic Epistles, there is no indication that the early Church turned her attention to sins of the past in order to ask for forgiveness. This might be explained by the powerful sense of the radical newness of Christianity, which tended to orient the community toward the future rather than the past.

There is, however, a more broad and subtle insistence pervading the New Testament: in the gospels and in the letters, the ambivalence of the Christian experience is fully recognized. For Paul, for example, the Christian community is an eschatological people that already lives the "new creation" (cf. 2 Cor 5:17; Gal 6:15), but this experience, made possible by the death and resurrection of Jesus (cf. Rom 3:21–26; 5:6–11; 8:1–11; 1 Cor 15:54–57), does not free us from the inclination to sin present in the world because of Adam's fall.

From the divine intervention in and through the death and resurrection of Jesus, it follows that there are now two scenarios possible: the history of Adam and the history of Christ. These proceed side by side and the believer must count on the death and resurrection of the Lord Jesus (cf., for example, Rom 6:1–11; Gal 3:27–28; Col 3:10; 2 Cor 5:14–15) to be part of the history in which "grace overflows" (cf. Rom 5:12–21).

A similar theological rereading of the paschal event of Christ shows how the early Church had an acute awareness of the possible deficiencies of the baptized. One could say that the entire *corpus paulinum* recalls believers to a full recognition of their dignity, albeit in the living awareness of the fragility of their human condition. "For freedom Christ set us free; so stand firm and do not submit again to the yoke of slavery" (Gal 5:1).

An analogous reason can be found in the gospel narratives. It arises decisively in Mark where the frailties of Jesus' disciples are one of the dominant themes of the account (cf. Mk 4:40–41; 6:36–37, 51–52; 8:14–21, 31–33; 9:5–6, 32–41; 10:32–45; 14:10–11, 17–21, 27–31, 50; 16:8). Even if understandably nuanced, the same motif recurs in all of the evangelists. Judas and Peter are respectively the traitor and the one who denies the Master, though Judas ends up in desperation for his act (cf. Acts 1:15–20), while Peter repents (cf. Lk 22:61) and arrives at a triple profession of love (cf. Jn 21:15–19). In Matthew, even during the final appearance of the risen Lord, while the disciples adore him, "some still doubted" (Mt 28:17). The Fourth Gospel presents the disciples as those to whom an incommensurable love was given even though their response was one of ignorance, deficiencies, denial and betrayal (cf. Jn 13:1–38).

This constant presentation of Jesus' disciples, who vacillate when it comes to yielding to sin, is not simply a critical rereading of the early history. The accounts are framed in such a way that they are addressed to every other disciple of Christ in difficulty who looks to the Gospel for guidance and inspiration. Moreover, the New Testament is full of exhortations to behave well, to live at a higher level of dedication, to avoid evil (cf., for example, Jas 1:5–8, 19–21; 2:1–7; 4:1–10; 1 Pt 1:13–25; 2 Pt 2:1–22; Jude 3:13; 1 Jn 5–10; 2:1–11; 18–27; 4:1–6; 2 Jn 7–11; 3 Jn 9–10).

There is, however, no explicit call addressed to the first Christians to confess the faults of the past, although the recognition of the reality of sin and evil within the Christian people—those called to the eschatological life proper to the Christian condition—is highly significant (it is enough to note the reproaches in the letters to the seven Churches in the Book of Revelation). According to the petition found in the Lord's Prayer, this people prays: "Forgive us our trespasses, as we forgive those who trespass against us" (Lk 11:4; cf. Mt 6:12).

Thus, the first Christians show that they are well aware that they could act in a way that does not correspond to their vocation, by not living their Baptism into the death and resurrection of Jesus.

2.3. The Biblical Jubilee

An important biblical precedent for reconciliation and overcoming of past situations is represented by the celebration of the Jubilee, as it is regulated in the Book of Leviticus (ch. 25). In a social structure made up of tribes, clans and families, situations of disorder were inevitably created when struggling individuals or families had to "redeem" themselves from their difficulties by consigning their land, house, servants or children to those who had more means than they had. Such a system resulted in some Israelites coming to suffer intolerable situations of debt, poverty and servitude in the same land that had been given to them by God, to the advantage of other children of Israel. All this could result in a territory or a clan falling into the hands of a few rich people for greater or lesser periods of time, while the rest of the families of the clan came to find themselves in a condition of debt or servitude, compelling them to live in total dependence upon a few well-off persons.

The legislation of Leviticus 25 constitutes an attempt to overturn this state of affairs (such that one could doubt whether it was ever put into practice fully). It convened the celebration of the Jubilee every fifty years in order to preserve the social fabric of the People of God and restore independence even to the smallest families of the country. Decisive for Leviticus 25 is the regular repetition of Israel's profession of faith in God who had liberated his people in the Exodus. "I, the Lord, am your God, who brought you out of the land of Egypt to give you the land of Canaan and to be your God" (Lv 25:38; cf. vv. 42, 45). The celebration of the Jubilee was an implicit admission of fault and an attempt to re-establish a just order. Any system which would alienate an Israelite—once a slave but now freed by the powerful arm of God—was in fact a denial of God's saving action in and through the Exodus.

The liberation of the victims and sufferers becomes part of the much broader program of the prophets. Deutero-Isaiah, in the Suffering Servant songs (Is 42:1–9; 49:1–6; 50:4–11; 52:13–53:12) develops these allusions to the practice of the Jubilee with the themes of ransom and of freedom, of return and redemption. Isaiah 58 is an attack on ritual observance that has no regard for social justice; it is a call for liberation of the oppressed (Is 58:6), centered specifically on the obligations of kinship (v.7). More clearly, Isaiah 61 uses the images of the Jubilee to depict the Anointed One as God's herald sent to "evangelize" the poor, to proclaim liberty to captives, and to announce the year of grace of the Lord. Significantly, it is precisely this text, with an allusion to Isaiah 58:6, that Jesus uses to present the task of his life and ministry in Luke 4:17–21.

2.4. Conclusion

From what has been said, it can be concluded that John Paul II's appeal to the Church to mark the Jubilee Year by an admission of guilt for the sufferings and wrongs committed by her sons and daughters in the past, as well as the ways in which this might be put into practice, do not find an exact parallel in the Bible. Nevertheless, they are based on what Sacred Scripture says about the holiness of God, the intergenerational solidarity of God's people, and the sinfulness of the people.

The Pope's appeal correctly captures the spirit of the biblical Jubilee, which calls for actions aimed at re-establishing the order of God's original plan for creation. This requires that the proclamation of the "today" of the Jubilee, begun by Jesus (cf. Lk 4:21), be continued in the Jubilee celebration of his Church. In addition, this singular experience of grace prompts the People of God as a whole, as well as each of the baptized, to take still greater cognizance of the mandate received from the Lord to be ever ready to forgive offenses received.[39]

---

39. Cf. *Tertio Millennio Adveniente,* 33–36.

3. Theological Foundations

"Hence it is appropriate that as the second millennium of Christianity draws to a close the Church should become ever more fully conscious of the sinfulness of her children, recalling all those times in history when they departed from the spirit of Christ and his Gospel and, instead of offering to the world the witness of a life inspired by the values of faith, indulged in ways of thinking and acting which were truly *forms of counterwitness and scandal.* Although she is holy because of her incorporation into Christ, the Church does not tire of doing penance. Before God and man, she always *acknowledges as her own her sinful sons and daughters.*"[40]

These words of John Paul II emphasize how the Church is touched by the sin of her children. She is holy in being made so by the Father through the sacrifice of the Son and the gift of the Spirit. She is also in a certain sense sinner, in really taking upon herself the sin of those whom she has generated in Bap-

---

40. *Tertio Millennio Adveniente,* 33.

tism. This is analogous to the way Christ Jesus took on the sin of the world (cf. Rom 8:3; 2 Cor 5:21; Gal 3:13; 1 Pt 2:24).[41]

Furthermore, in her most profound self-awareness in time, the Church knows that she is not only a community of the elect, but one which in her very bosom includes both righteous and sinners, of the present as well as the past, in the unity of the mystery which constitutes her. Indeed, in grace and in the woundedness of sin, the baptized of today are close to, and in solidarity with, those of yesterday. For this reason one can say that the Church—one in time and space in Christ and in the Spirit—is truly "at the same time holy and ever in need of purification."[42] It is from this paradox, which is characteristic of the mystery of the Church, that the question arises as to how one can reconcile the two aspects: on the one hand, the Church's affirmation in faith of her holiness, and on the other hand, her unceasing need for penance and purification.

3.1. The Mystery of the Church

"The Church is in history, but at the same time she transcends it. It is only 'with the eyes of faith' that one can see her in her visible reality and at the same time in her spiritual reality as bearer of divine life."[43] The ensemble of her visible and historical aspects stands in relation to the divine gift in a way

41. One thinks of the reason why Christian authors of various historical periods reproached the Church for her faults. Among these, one of the most representative examples is the *Liber Asceticus* by Maximus the Confessor: *PL* 90, 912–956.

42. *Lumen Gentium,* 8.

43. *Catechism of the Catholic Church,* 770.

that is analogous to how, in the incarnate Word of God, the assumed humanity is sign and instrument of the action of the divine Person of the Son.

The two dimensions of ecclesial being form "one complex reality resulting from a human and a divine element,"[44] in a communion that participates in the Trinitarian life and brings about baptized persons' sense of being united among themselves despite historical differences of time and place. By the power of this communion, the Church presents herself as a subject that is absolutely unique in human affairs, able to take on the gifts, the merits, and the faults of her children of yesterday and today.

The telling analogy to the mystery of the incarnate Word implies too, nevertheless, a fundamental difference. "Christ, 'holy, innocent, and undefiled' (Heb 7:26), knew no sin (cf. 2 Cor 5:21), but came only to expiate the sins of the people (cf. Heb 2:17). The Church, however, embracing sinners in her bosom, is at the same time holy and always in need of purification and incessantly pursues the path of penance and renewal."[45]

The absence of sin in the incarnate Word cannot be attributed to his ecclesial Body, within which, on the contrary, each person—participating in the grace bestowed by God—needs nevertheless to be vigilant and to be continually purified. Each member also shares in the weakness of others: "All members of the Church, including her ministers, must acknowledge that

44. *Lumen Gentium,* 8.

45. *Ibid.* Cf. also *Unitatis Redintegratio,* 3 and 6.

they are sinners (cf. 1 Jn 1:8–10). In everyone, the weeds of sin will still be mixed with the good wheat of the Gospel until the end of time (cf. Mt 13:24–30). Hence the Church gathers sinners already caught up in Christ's salvation but still on the way to holiness."[46]

Already Paul VI had solemnly affirmed that the Church "is holy, though she includes sinners in her bosom, for she herself has no other life but the life of grace.... This is why she suffers and does penance for these faults, from which she has the power to free her children through the blood of Christ and the gift of the Holy Spirit."[47] The Church in her "mystery" is thus the encounter of sanctity and of weakness, continually redeemed, and yet always in need of the power of redemption. As the liturgy—the true *"lex credendi"*—teaches, the individual Christian and the community of the saints implore God to look upon the faith of his Church and not on the sins of individuals, which are the negation of this living faith: *"Ne respicias peccata nostra, sed fidem Ecclesiae tuae!"* In the unity of the mystery of the Church through time and space, it is possible to consider the aspect of holiness, the need for repentance and reform, and their articulation in the actions of Mother Church.

3.2. The Holiness of the Church

The Church is holy because, sanctified by Christ who has acquired her by giving himself up to death for her, she is maintained in holiness by the Holy Spirit who pervades her unceasingly:

46. *Catechism of the Catholic Church,* 827.

47. Paul VI, *Credo of the People of God* (June 30, 1968), 19 (*Enchiridion Vaticanum* 3, 264 f.).

"We believe that the Church...is indefectibly holy. For Christ, the Son of God, who with the Father and the Spirit is praised as being 'alone holy,' loved the Church as his bride and gave himself up for her, so that she might be made holy (cf. Eph 5:25), and has united her to himself as his body and has filled her with the gift of the Holy Spirit, to the glory of God. For this reason, everyone in the Church...is called to holiness."[48]

In this sense, from the beginning, the members of the Church are called the "saints" (cf. Acts 9:13; 1 Cor 6:1; 16:1). One can distinguish, however, the *holiness of the Church* from *holiness in the Church.* The former—founded on the missions of the Son and Spirit—guarantees the continuity of the mission of the People of God until the end of time and stimulates and aids the believers in pursuing subjective personal holiness. The form which holiness takes is rooted in the vocation that each one receives; it is given and required of him as the full completion of his own vocation and mission. Personal holiness is always directed toward God and others, and thus has an essentially social character: it is holiness "in the Church" oriented toward the good of all.

Holiness *in* the Church must therefore correspond to the holiness *of* the Church. "The followers of Christ, called by God not according to their works, but according to his own purpose and grace, and justified in the Lord Jesus, have been made truly children of God in the Baptism of faith and sharers in the divine nature, and thus are really made holy. They must there-

---

48. *Lumen Gentium,* 39.

fore hold on to and perfect in their lives that sanctification which they have received from God."[49]

The baptized person is called to become with his entire existence that which he has already become by virtue of his baptismal consecration. And this does not happen without the consent of his freedom and the assistance of the grace that comes from God. No one becomes himself so fully as does the saint, who welcomes the divine plan and, with the help of grace, conforms his entire being to it! The saints are in this sense like lights kindled by the Lord in the midst of his Church in order to illuminate her; they are a prophecy for the whole world.

3.3. The Necessity of Continual Renewal

Without obscuring this holiness, we must acknowledge that due to the presence of sin there is a need for continual renewal and for constant conversion in the People of God. The Church on earth is "marked with a true holiness," which is, however, "imperfect."[50] Augustine observes against the Pelagians: "The Church as a whole says: Forgive us our trespasses! Therefore she has blemishes and wrinkles. But by means of confession the wrinkles are smoothed away and the blemishes washed clean. The Church stands in prayer in order to be purified by confession, and as long as men live on earth it will be so."[51]

---

49. *Ibid.,* 40.
50. *Ibid.,* 48.
51. St. Augustine, *Sermo* 181, 5, 7: *PL* 38; 982.

And Thomas Aquinas makes clear that the fullness of holiness belongs to eschatological time; in the meantime, the Church still on pilgrimage should not deceive herself by saying that she is without sin: "To be a glorious Church, with neither spot nor wrinkle, is the ultimate end to which we are brought by the Passion of Christ. Hence, this will be the case only in the heavenly homeland, not here on the way of pilgrimage, where 'if we say we have no sin we deceive ourselves.'"[52]

In reality, "though we are clothed with the baptismal garment, we do not cease to sin, to turn away from God. Now, in this new petition ['forgive us our trespasses'], we return to him like the prodigal son (cf. Lk 15:11–32) and, like the tax collector, recognize that we are sinners before him (cf. Lk 18:13). Our petition begins with a 'confession' of our wretchedness and his mercy."[53]

Hence it is the entire Church that confesses her faith in God through the confession of her children's sins and celebrates his infinite goodness and capacity for forgiveness. Thanks to the bond established by the Holy Spirit, the communion that exists among all the baptized in time and space is such that in this communion each person is himself, but at the same time is conditioned by others and exercises an influence on them in the living exchange of spiritual goods. In this way, the holiness of each one influences the growth in goodness of others; however, sin also does not have an exclusively individual relevance, because it burdens and poses resistance along the way of salva-

52. St. Thomas Aquinas, *Summa Theol.*, III, q. 8, art. 3, *ad* 2.
53. *Catechism of the Catholic Church,* 2839.

tion of all and, in this sense, truly touches the Church in her entirety, across the various times and places.

This distinction prompts the Fathers to make sharp statements like this one of Ambrose: "Let us beware then that our fall not become a wound of the Church."[54] The Church therefore, "although she is holy because of her incorporation into Christ... does not tire of doing penance. Before God and man, she always acknowledges as her own her sinful sons and daughters"[55] of both yesterday and today.

3.4. The Motherhood of the Church

The conviction that the Church can make herself responsible for the sin of her children by virtue of the solidarity that exists among them through time and space because of their incorporation into Christ and the work of the Holy Spirit, is expressed in a particularly effective way in the idea of "Mother Church" *(Mater Ecclesia),* which "in the conception of the early Fathers of the Church sums up the entire Christian aspiration."[56]

The Church, Vatican II affirms, "by means of the Word of God faithfully received, becomes a mother, since through

---

54. St. Ambrose, *De Virginitate* 8, 48; *PL* 16, 278D: *"Caveamus igitur, ne lapsus noster vulnus Ecclesiae fiat." Lumen Gentium* 11 also speaks of the wound inflicted on the Church by the sins of her children.

55. *Tertio Millennio Adveniente,* 33.

56. Karl Delahaye, *Ecclesia Mater chez les Pères des trois premiers siècles* (Paris, 1964), 128; cf. also Hugo Rahner, SJ, *Mater Ecclesia: Lobpreis der Kirche aus dem ersten Jahrtausend christlicher Literatur* (Einsiedeln, 1944).

preaching and baptism she brings forth children to a new and immortal life, who have been conceived by the Holy Spirit and born of God."[57] Augustine, for example, gives voice to the vast tradition, of which these ideas are an echo: "This holy and honored mother is like Mary. She gives birth and she is a virgin, from her you were born—she generates Christ so that you will be members of Christ."[58] Cyprian of Carthage states succinctly: "One cannot have God as a father who does not have the Church as a mother."[59] And Paulinus of Nola sings of the motherhood of the Church like this: "As a mother she receives the seed of the eternal Word, carries the peoples in her womb and gives birth to them."[60]

According to this vision, the Church is continually realized in the exchange and communication of the Spirit from one believer to another, as the generative environment of faith and holiness, in fraternal communion, unanimity in prayer, solidarity with the cross, and common witness. By virtue of this living communication, each baptized person can be considered to be

57. *Lumen Gentium,* 64.

58. St. Augustine, *Sermo* 25, 8: *PL* 46, 938: *"Mater ista sancta, honorata, Mariae similis, et parit et Virgo est. Ex illa nati estis et Christum parit: nam membra Christi estis."*

59. St. Cyprian, *De Ecclesiae Catholicae Unitate* 6: *CCL* 3, 253: *"Habere iam non potest Deum patrem qui ecclesiam non habet matrem."* St. Cyprian also states: *"Ut habere quis possit Deum Patrem, habeat ante ecclesiam matrem"* (*Epist.* 74, 7; *CCL* 3C, 572). St. Augustine: *"Tenete ergo, carissimi, tenete omnes unanimiter Deum patrem, et matrem Ecclesiam"* (*In Ps 88, Sermo* 2, 14: *CCL* 39, 1244).

60. St. Paulinus of Nola, *Carmen* 25, 171–172; *CSEL* 30, 243: *"Inde manet mater aeterni semine verbi / concipiens populos et pariter pariens."*

at the same time a child of the Church, in that he is generated in her to divine life, and Mother Church, in that, by his faith and love he cooperates in giving birth to new children for God. He is ever more Mother Church, the greater is his holiness and the more ardent is his effort to communicate to others the gift he has received.

On the other hand, the baptized person does not cease to be a child of the Church when, because of sin, he separates himself from her in his heart. He may always come back to the springs of grace and remove the burden that his sin imposes on the entire community of Mother Church. The Church, in turn, as a true Mother, cannot but be wounded by the sins of her children of yesterday and today, continuing to love them always, to the point of making herself responsible in all times for the burden created by their sins. Thus, she is seen by the Fathers of the Church to be the Mother of sorrows, not only because of persecutions coming from outside, but above all because of the betrayals, failures, delays and sinfulness of her children.

Holiness and sin *in* the Church are reflected therefore in their effects on the entire Church, although it is a conviction of faith that holiness is stronger than sin, since it is the fruit of divine grace. The saints are shining proof of this, and are recognized as models and help for all! There is no parallelism between grace and sin, nor even a kind of symmetry or dialectical relationship. The influence of evil will never be able to conquer the force of grace and the radiance of good, even the most hidden good! In this sense the Church recognizes herself to be holy in her saints.

While she rejoices over this holiness and knows its benefit, she nonetheless confesses herself a sinner, not as a subject who sins, but rather in assuming the weight of her children's faults in maternal solidarity, so as to cooperate in overcoming them through penance and newness of life. For this reason, the holy Church recognizes the duty "to express profound regret for the weaknesses of so many of her sons and daughters who sullied her face, preventing her from fully mirroring the image of her crucified Lord, the supreme witness of patient love and humble meekness."[61]

This expression of regret can be done in a particular way by those who by charism and ministry express the communion of the People of God in its weightiest form: on behalf of the local Churches, bishops may be able to make confessions for wrongs and requests for forgiveness. For the entire Church, one in time and space, the person capable of speaking is he who exercises the universal ministry of unity, the Bishop of the Church "which presides in love,"[62] the Pope. This is why it is particularly significant that the invitation came from him that "the Church should become more fully conscious of the sinfulness of her children" and recognize the necessity "to make amends for...[the sins of the past], and earnestly beseech Christ's forgiveness."[63]

---

61. *Tertio Millennio Adveniente,* 35.

62. St. Ignatius of Antioch, *Ad Romanos, Prooem.: SC* 10, 124 (Th. Camelot, Paris, 1958).

63. *Tertio Millennio Adveniente,* 33, 34.

4. Historical Judgment and Theological Judgment

The determination of the wrongs of the past, for which amends are to be made, implies, first of all, a correct historical judgment, which is also the foundation of the theological evaluation. One must ask: What precisely occurred? What exactly was said and done? Only when these questions are adequately answered through rigorous historical analysis can one then ask whether what happened, what was said or done, can be understood as consistent with the Gospel, and, if it cannot, whether the Church's sons and daughters who acted in such a way could have recognized this, given the context in which they acted. Only when there is moral certainty that what was done in contradiction to the Gospel in the name of the Church by certain of her sons and daughters could have been understood by them as such and avoided, can it have significance for the Church of today to make amends for faults of the past.

The relationship between "historical judgment" and "theological judgment" is therefore as complex as it is necessary and determinative. For this reason, it is necessary to undertake it without falsehoods on one side or the other. Both an apologetics that seeks to justify everything and an unwarranted laying of blame, based on historically untenable attributions of responsibility, must be avoided.

John Paul II, referring to the historical-theological evaluation of the work of the Inquisition, stated: "The Church's Magisterium certainly may not intend to perform an act of natural ethics, which the request for pardon is, without first being exactly informed concerning the situation of that time. But, at the same time, neither may it rely on images of the past steered by public opinion, since these are frequently highly charged with passionate emotion which impedes serene and objective diagnosis.... This is the reason why the first step consists in asking the historians, not to furnish a judgment of natural ethics, which would exceed the area of their competence, but to offer help toward a reconstruction, as precise as possible, of the events, of the customs, of the mentality of the time, in the light of the historical context of the epoch."[64]

4.1. The Interpretation of History

What are the conditions for a correct interpretation of the past from the point of view of historical knowledge? To determine these, we must take account of the complexity of the relationship between the subject who interprets and the object from the past which is interpreted.[65]

---

64. *Discourse* to the participants in the International Symposium of study on the Inquisition, sponsored by the Historical-Theological Commission of the Central Committee of the Jubilee, n. 4; October 31, 1998.

65. Cf. for what follows, Hans-Georg Gadamer, *Wahrheit und Methode,* 2nd ed. (Tübingen, 1965); Eng. trans. *Truth and Method* (London: Sheed and Ward, 1975).

First, their mutual extraneousness must be emphasized. Events or words of the past are, above all, "past." As such they are not completely reducible to the framework of the present, but possess an objective density and complexity that prevent them from being ordered in a solely functional way for present interests. It is necessary, therefore, to approach them by means of a historical-critical investigation that aims at using all of the information available, with a view to a reconstruction of the environment, of the ways of thinking, of the conditions and the living dynamic in which those events and those words are placed, in order, in such a way, to ascertain the contents and the challenges that—precisely in their diversity—they propose to our present time.

Second, a certain *common belonging* of interpreter and interpreted must be recognized without which no bond and no communication could exist between past and present. This communicative bond is based on the fact that every human being, whether of yesterday or of today, is situated in a complex of historical relationships, and in order to live these relationships, the mediation of language is necessary, a mediation which itself is always historically determined. Everybody belongs to history!

Bringing to light this communality between interpreter and the object of interpretation—which is reached through the multiple forms by which the past leaves evidence of itself (texts, monuments, traditions, etc.)—means judging both the accuracy of possible correspondences and possible difficulties of communication between past and present, as indicated by one's own understanding of the past words and events. This requires taking into account the questions which motivate the research and their effect on the answers which are found, the living context in which the work is undertaken, and the interpreting community whose language is spoken and to whom one intends to speak. For this purpose, it is necessary that the pre-understanding—which is part of every act of interpretation—be as reflective and conscious as possible, in order to measure and moderate its real effect on the interpretative process.

Finally, through the effort to know and to evaluate, an *osmosis* (a "fusion of horizons") is accomplished between the interpreter and the object of the past that is interpreted, in which the act of comprehension properly consists. This is the expression of what is judged to be the correct understanding of the events or words of the past; it is equivalent to grasping the meaning which the events can have for the interpreter and his world. Thanks to this encounter of living worlds, understanding of the past is translated into its application to the present. The past is grasped in the potentialities which it discloses, in the stimulus it offers to modify the present. Memory becomes capable of giving rise to a new future.

This fruitful *osmosis* with the past is reached through the interwovenness of certain basic hermeneutic operations, which correspond to the stages of extraneousness, communality, and understanding true and proper. In relation to a "text" of the past (understood in a general sense as evidence which may be written, oral, monumental or figurative), these operations can be expressed as follows: "1) understanding the text; 2) judging how correct one's understanding of the text is; and 3) stating what one judges to be the correct understanding of the text."[66]

---

66. Bernard Lonergan, SJ, *Method in Theology,* (London, 1972), 155.

Understanding the evidence of the past means reaching it as far as possible in its objectivity through all the sources that are available. Judging the correctness of one's own interpretation means verifying honestly and rigorously to what extent it could have been oriented or conditioned in any way by one's prior understanding or by possible prejudices. Stating the interpretation reached means bringing others into the dialogue created with the past, in order both to verify its importance and to discover other possible interpretations.

4.2. Historical Investigation and Theological Evaluation

If these operations are present in every hermeneutic act, they must also be part of the interpretative process within which historical judgment and theological judgment come to be integrated. This requires, in the first place, that in this type of interpretation, maximum attention be given to the elements of differentiation and extraneousness between past and present.

In particular, when one intends to judge the possible wrongs of the past, it must be kept in mind that the historical periods are different, that the sociological and cultural times within which the Church acts are different, and so, the paradigms and judgments proper to one society and to one era might be applied erroneously in the evaluation of other periods of history, producing many misunderstandings. Persons, institutions and their respective competencies are different; ways of thinking and conditioning are different. Therefore, responsibility for what was said and done has to be precisely identified, taking into account the fact that the Church's request for forgiveness commits the single theological subject of the Church in the variety of ways and levels in which she is represented by individual persons and in the enormous diversity of historical and geographical situations. Generalization must be avoided. Any possible statement today must be situated in the contemporary context and undertaken by the appropriate subject (universal Church, bishops of a country, particular Churches, etc.).

Second, the correlation of historical judgment and theological judgment must take into account the fact that, for the interpretation of the faith, the bond between past and present is not motivated only by the current interest and by the common belonging of every human being to history and its expressive mediations, but is based also on the unifying action of the Spirit of God and on the permanent identity of the constitutive principle of the communion of the faithful, which is revelation. The Church—by virtue of the communion produced in her by the Spirit of Christ in time and space—cannot fail to recognize herself in her supernatural aspect, present and operative in all times, as a subject in a certain way unique, called to correspond to the gift of God in different forms and situations through the choices of her children, despite all of the deficiencies that may have characterized them.

Communion in the one Holy Spirit also establishes a communion of "saints" in a diachronic sense, by virtue of which the baptized of today feel connected to the baptized of yesterday and—as they benefit from their merits and are nourished by their witness of holiness—so likewise they feel the obligation to assume any current burden from their faults, after having discerned these by attentive historical and theological study.

Thanks to this objective and transcendent foundation of the communion of the People of God in its various historical situations, interpretation done by believers recognizes in the Church's past a very particular significance for the present day.

The encounter with the past, produced in the act of interpretation, can have particular value for the present, and be rich in a "performative" efficaciousness that cannot always be calculated beforehand.

Of course, the powerful unity between the hermeneutic horizon and the Church as interpreting agent exposes the theological vision to the risk of yielding to apologetic or tendentious readings. It is here that the hermeneutic exercise aimed at understanding past events and statements and at evaluating the correctness of their interpretation for today is more necessary than ever. For this reason, the reading undertaken by believers will avail itself of all possible contributions by the historical sciences and interpretative methods.

The exercise of historical hermeneutics should not, however, prevent the evaluation of faith from questioning the texts according to its own distinctive vision, thus making past and present interact in the conscience of the one fundamental subject involved in these texts, the Church. This guards against all historicism that would relativize the weight of past wrongs and make history justify everything. As John Paul II observes, "an accurate historical judgment cannot prescind from careful study of the cultural conditioning of the times.... Yet the consideration of mitigating factors does not exonerate the Church from the obligation to express profound regret for the weaknesses of so many of her sons and daughters...."[67]

The Church is "not afraid of the truth that emerges from history and is ready to acknowledge mistakes wherever they

67. *Tertio Millennio Adveniente,* 35.

have been identified, especially when they involve the respect that is owed to individuals and communities. She is inclined to mistrust generalizations that excuse or condemn various historical periods. She entrusts the investigation of the past to patient, honest, scholarly reconstruction, free from confessional or ideological prejudices, regarding both the accusations brought against her and the wrongs she has suffered."[68] The examples offered in the following chapter may furnish a concrete demonstration.

---

68. John Paul II, *General Audience Discourse* of September 1, 1999; in *L'Osservatore Romano,* Eng. ed., September 8, 1999, 7.

5. Ethical Discernment

In order for the Church to carry out an appropriate historical examination of conscience before God with a view to her own interior renewal and growth in grace and holiness, it is necessary that she recognize the "forms of counterwitness and of scandal" that have taken place in her history, especially in the past millennium. It is not possible to undertake such a task without being aware of its moral and spiritual significance. This entails defining some key terms, as well as making some necessary ethical clarifications.

5.1. Some Ethical Criteria

On the level of morality, the request for forgiveness always presupposes an admission of *responsibility,* precisely the responsibility for a wrong committed against others. Usually, *moral responsibility* refers to the relationship between the action and the person who does it. It establishes who is responsible for an act, its attribution to a certain person or persons. The responsibility may be *objective* or *subjective.* Objective responsibility refers to the moral value of the act in itself, insofar as it is good or evil, and thus refers to the imputability of the action. Subjective responsibility concerns the effective perception by individual conscience of the goodness or evil of the act performed.

Subjective responsibility ceases with the death of the one who performed the act; it is not transmitted through generation; the descendants do not inherit (subjective) responsibility for the acts of their ancestors. In this sense, asking for forgiveness presupposes a contemporaneity between those who are hurt by an action and those who committed it. The only responsibility capable of continuing in history can be the objective kind, to which one may freely adhere subjectively or not. Thus, the evil done often outlives the one who did it through the consequences of behaviors that can become a heavy burden on the consciences and memories of the descendants.

In such a context, one can speak of a *solidarity* that unites the past and the present in a relationship of reciprocity. In certain situations, the burden that weighs on conscience can be so heavy as to constitute a kind of moral and religious memory of the evil done, which is by its nature a *common memory.* This common memory gives eloquent testimony to the solidarity objectively existing between those who committed the evil in the past and their heirs in the present. It is then that it becomes possible to speak of an *objective common responsibility.* Liberation from the weight of this responsibility comes above all through imploring God's forgiveness for the wrongs of the past, and then, where appropriate, through the "purification of memory" culminating in a mutual pardoning of sins and offenses in the present.

Purifying the memory means eliminating from personal and collective conscience all forms of resentment or violence left by the inheritance of the past, on the basis of a new and rigorous historical-theological judgment, which becomes the foundation for a renewed moral way of acting. This occurs whenever it becomes possible to attribute to past historical deeds a different quality, having a new and different effect on the present, in view of progress in reconciliation in truth, justice and charity among human beings and, in particular, between the Church and the different religious, cultural and civil communities with whom she is related.

Emblematic models of such an effect, which a later authoritative interpretative judgment may have for the entire life of the Church, are the reception of the Councils or acts like the abolition of mutual anathemas. These express a new assessment of past history, which is capable of producing a different characterization of the relationships lived in the present. The memory of division and opposition is purified and substituted by a reconciled memory, to which everyone in the Church is invited to be open to and to become educated in its regard.

The combination of historical judgment and theological judgment in the process of interpreting the past is connected to the ethical repercussions that it may have in the present and entails some principles corresponding, on the moral plane, to the hermeneutic foundation of the relationship between historical judgment and theological judgment. These are:

a. The principle of conscience. Conscience, as "moral judgment" and as "moral imperative," constitutes the final evaluation of an act as good or evil before God. In effect, only God knows the moral value of each human act, even if the Church, like Jesus, can and must classify, judge and sometimes condemn some kinds of action (cf. Mt 18:15–18).

b. The principle of historicity. Precisely inasmuch as every human act belongs to the subject who acts, every individual conscience and every society chooses and acts within a determined horizon of time and space. To truly understand human acts or their related dynamics, we need therefore to enter into the world of those who did them. Only in such a way can we come to know their motivations and their moral principles. This must be said without prejudice to the solidarity that binds the members of a specific community through the passage of time.

c. The principle of "paradigm change." While before the Enlightenment there existed a sort of osmosis between Church and State, between faith and culture, morality and law, from the eighteenth century onward this relationship was modified significantly. The result was a transition from a sacral society to a pluralist society, or as occurred in a few cases, to a secular society. The models of thought and action, the so-called "paradigms" of actions and evaluation, change. Such a transition has a direct impact on moral judgments, although this influence does not justify in any way a relativistic idea of moral principles or of the nature of morality itself.

The entire process of purification of memory, however, insofar as it requires the correct combination of historical evaluation and theological perception, needs to be lived by the Church's sons and daughters not only with the rigor that takes account of the criteria and principles indicated above, but is also accompanied by a continual calling upon the help of the Holy Spirit. This is necessary in order not to fall into resentment or unwarranted self-recrimination, but to arrive instead at the confession of the God whose "mercy is from age to age" (Lk 1:50), who wants life and not death, forgiveness and not condemnation, love and not fear.

The quality of *exemplarity* which the honest admission of past faults can exert on attitudes within the Church and civil society should also be noted, for it gives rise to a renewed obedience to the truth and to respect for the dignity and the rights of others, most especially, of the very weak. In this sense, the numerous requests for forgiveness formulated by John Paul II constitute an example that draws attention to something good and stimulates the imitation of it, recalling individuals and groups of people to an honest and fruitful examination of conscience with a view to reconciliation.

In the light of these ethical clarifications, we can now explore some examples—among which are those mentioned in *Tertio Millennio Adveniente*[69]—of situations in which the behavior of the sons and daughters of the Church seems to have contradicted the Gospel of Jesus Christ in a significant way.

5.2. The Division of Christians

Unity is the law of the life of the Trinitarian God revealed to the world by the Son (cf. Jn 17:21), who, in the power of the Holy Spirit, loving until the end (cf. Jn 13:1), communicates this life to his own. This unity should be the source and the form of the communion of mankind's life with the Triune God. If Christians live this law of mutual love, so as to be one "as the Father and the Son are one," the result will be that "the world will believe that the Son was sent by the Father" (Jn 17:21) and "everyone will know that these are his disciples" (Jn 13:35).

---

69. Cf. *Tertio Millennio Adveniente,* 34–36.

Unfortunately, it has not happened this way, particularly in the millennium which has just ended and in which great divisions appeared among Christians, in open contradiction to the explicit will of Christ, as if he himself were divided (cf. 1 Cor 1:13). Vatican Council II judges this fact in this way: "Certainly such division openly contradicts the will of Christ, is a scandal to the world, and damages that most holy cause, the preaching of the Gospel to every creature."[70]

The principal divisions during the past millennium which "affect the seamless garment of Christ"[71] are the schism between the Eastern and Western Churches at the beginning of this millennium, and in the West—four centuries later—the laceration caused by those events "commonly referred to as the Reformation."[72] It is true that "these various divisions differ greatly from one another not only by reason of their origin, place and time, but above all by reason of the nature and gravity of questions concerning faith and the structure of the Church."[73]

In the schism of the eleventh century, cultural and historical factors played an important role, while the doctrinal dimension concerned the authority of the Church and the Bishop of Rome, a topic which at that time had not reached the clarity it has today, thanks to the doctrinal development of this millen-

70. *Unitatis Redintegratio,* 1.

71. *Ibid.,* 13. *Tertio Millennio Adveniente* 34 states that "In the course of the thousand years now drawing to a close, even more than in the first millennium, ecclesial communion has been painfully wounded...."

72. *Unitatis Redintegratio,* 13.

73. *Ibid.*

nium. In the case of the Reformation, however, other areas of revelation and doctrine were objects of controversy.

The way that has opened to overcome these differences is that of doctrinal development animated by mutual love. The lack of supernatural love, of *agape,* seems to have been common to both breaches. Given that this charity is the supreme commandment of the Gospel, without which all the rest is but "a noisy gong or a clanging cymbal" (1 Cor 13:1), such a deficiency needs to be seen in all its seriousness before the Risen One, the Lord of the Church and of history. It is by virtue of the recognition of this lack that Pope Paul VI asked pardon of God and of the "separated brethren," who may have felt offended "by us" (the Catholic Church).[74]

In 1965, in the climate produced by the Second Vatican Council, Patriarch Athenagoras, in his dialogue with Paul VI, emphasized the theme of the restoration *(apokatastasis)* of mutual love, so essential after a history laden with opposition, mutual mistrust, and antagonism.[75] It was a question of a past that, through memory, was still exerting its influence. The events of 1965 (culminating on December 7, 1965, with the abolition of the anathemas of 1054 between East and West) represent a confession of the fault contained in the earlier mutual exclusion, so as to purify the memory of the past and generate a new one.

---

74. Cf. *Opening Speech* of the Second Session of the Second Vatican Council (September 29, 1964): *Enchiridion Vaticanum* 1, [106], n. 176.

75. Cf. the documentation from the dialogue of charity between the Holy See and the Ecumenical Patriarch of Constantinople in *Tómos Agápes: Vatican—Phanar (1958–1970),* (Rome—Istanbul, 1971).

The basis of this *new memory* cannot be other than mutual love or, better, the renewed commitment to live it. This is the commandment *ante omnia* (1 Pt 4:8) for the Church in the East and in the West. In such a way, memory frees us from the prison of the past and calls Catholics and Orthodox, as well as Catholics and Protestants, to be the architects of a future more in conformity with the new commandment. Pope Paul VI's and Patriarch Athenagoras' testimony to this new memory is in this sense exemplary.

Particularly problematic for the path toward the unity of Christians is the temptation to be guided—or even determined—by cultural factors, historical conditioning and those prejudices which feed the separation and mutual distrust among Christians, even though they do not have anything to do with matters of faith. The Church's sons and daughters should sincerely examine their consciences to see whether they are actively committed to obeying the imperative of unity and are living an "interior conversion," because "it is from newness of attitudes of mind (cf. Eph 4:23), from self-denial and generous love, that desires for unity take their rise and grow toward maturity."[76]

In the period from the close of the Council until today, resistance to its message has certainly saddened the Spirit of God (cf. Eph 4:30). To the extent that some Catholics are pleased to remain bound to the separations of the past, doing nothing to remove the obstacles that impede unity, one could justly speak of solidarity in the sin of division (cf. 1 Cor 1:10–16). In this context the words of the *Decree on Ecumenism*

76. *Unitatis Redintegratio*, 7.

could be recalled: "With humble prayer we ask pardon of God and of the separated brethren, as we forgive those who trespass against us."[77]

5.3. The Use of Force in the Service of Truth

To the counterwitness of the division between Christians should be added that of the various occasions in the past millennium when doubtful means were employed in the pursuit of good ends, such as the proclamation of the Gospel or the defense of the unity of the faith. "Another sad chapter of history to which the sons and daughters of the Church must return with a spirit of repentance is that of the acquiescence given, especially in certain centuries, to intolerance and even the use of force in the service of truth."[78] This refers to forms of evangelization that employed improper means to announce the revealed truth, or did not include an evangelical discernment suited to the cultural values of peoples, or did not respect the consciences of the persons to whom the faith was presented, as well as all forms of force used in the repression and correction of errors.

Analogous attention should be paid to all the failures, for which the sons and daughters of the Church may have been responsible, to denounce injustice and violence in the great variety of historical situations: "Then there is the lack of discernment by many Christians in situations where basic human rights were violated. The request for forgiveness applies to whatever should have been done or was passed over in silence

---

77. *Ibid.*

78. *Tertio Millennio Adveniente,* 35.

because of weakness or bad judgment, to what was done or said hesitantly or inappropriately."[79]

As always, establishing the historical truth by means of historical-critical research is decisive. Once the facts have been established, it will be necessary to evaluate their spiritual and moral value, as well as their objective significance. Only thus will it be possible to avoid every form of mythical memory and reach a fair critical memory capable—in the light of faith—of producing fruits of conversion and renewal.

"From these painful moments of the past a lesson can be drawn for the future, leading all Christians to adhere fully to the sublime principle stated by the Council: 'The truth cannot impose itself except by virtue of its own truth, as it wins over the mind with both gentleness and power.'"[80]

5.4. Christians and Jews

The relationship between Christians and Jews is one of the areas requiring a special examination of conscience.[81] "The Church's relationship to the Jewish people is unlike the one she shares with any other religion."[82] Nevertheless, "the history of

---

79. John Paul II, *General Audience Discourse* of September 1, 1999; in *L'Osservatore Romano,* Eng. ed., September 8, 1999, 7.

80. *Tertio Millennio Adveniente,* 35. The citation from the Second Vatican Council is from *Dignitatis Humanae,* 1.

81. The argument is rigorously treated in the Declaration of the Second Vatican Council, *Nostra Aetate.*

82. Commission for Religious Relations with the Jews, *We Remember: A Reflection on the Shoah,* Rome (March 16, 1998), I, in *Information Service* of the Pontifical Council for Promoting Christian Unity, n. 97, 19. Cf. John Paul II, *Discourse at the Synagogue of Rome,* April 13, 1986; *AAS* 78 (1986), 1120.

the relations between Jews and Christians is a tormented one.... In effect, the balance of these relations over two thousand years has been quite negative."[83]

The hostility or diffidence of numerous Christians toward Jews in the course of time is a sad historical fact and is the cause of profound remorse for Christians aware of the fact that "Jesus was a descendent of David; that the Virgin Mary and the apostles belonged to the Jewish people; that the Church draws sustenance from the root of that good olive tree onto which have been grafted the wild olive branches of the Gentiles (cf. Rom 11:17–24); that the Jews are our dearly beloved brothers, indeed in a certain sense they are 'our elder brothers.'"[84]

The Shoah was certainly the result of the pagan ideology that was Nazism, animated by a merciless anti-Semitism that not only despised the faith of the Jewish people, but also denied their very human dignity. Nevertheless, "it may be asked whether the Nazi persecution of the Jews was not made easier by the anti-Jewish prejudices imbedded in some Christian minds and hearts.... Did Christians give every possible assistance to those being persecuted, and in particular to the persecuted Jews?"[85]

There is no doubt that there were many Christians who risked their lives to save and to help their Jewish neighbors. It

---

83. This is the judgment of the recent document of the Commission for Religious Relations with the Jews, *We Remember: A Reflection on the Shoah,* Rome (March 16, 1998), III, in *Information Service* of the Pontifical Council for Promoting Christian Unity, n. 97, 19.

84. *Ibid.,* V, 22.

85. *Ibid.,* IV, 20, 21.

seems, however, also true that "alongside such courageous men and women, the spiritual resistance and concrete action of other Christians was not that which might have been expected from Christ's followers."[86]

This fact constitutes a call to the consciences of all Christians today, so as to require "an act of repentance *(teshuva),*"[87] and to be a stimulus to increase efforts to be "transformed by the renewal of your mind" (Rom 12:2), as well as to keep a "moral and religious memory" of the injury inflicted on the Jews. In this area, much has already been done, but this should be confirmed and deepened.

5.5. Our Responsibility for the Evils of Today

"The present age in fact, together with much light, also presents not a few shadows."[88] First among the latter, we might mention the phenomenon of the denial of God in its many forms. What is particularly apparent is that this denial, especially in its more theoretical aspects, is a process that emerged in the Western world. Connected to the eclipse of God, one encounters a series of negative phenomena, like religious indifference, the widespread lack of a transcendent sense of human life, a climate of secularism and ethical relativism, the denial of the right to life of the unborn child sanctioned in pro-abortion legislation, and a great indifference to the cry of the poor in entire sectors of the human family.

---

86. *Ibid.,* IV, 21.

87. *Ibid.,* V, 22.

88. *Tertio Millennio Adveniente,* 36.

The uncomfortable question to consider is in what measure believers are themselves responsible for these forms of atheism, whether theoretical or practical. *Gaudium et Spes* responds with well-chosen words: "Believers themselves often share some responsibility for this situation. For, taken as a whole, atheism is not something original, but rather stems from a variety of causes, including a critical reaction against religious belief and in some places against the Christian religion in particular. Hence believers can have more than a little to do with the genesis of atheism."[89]

The true face of God has been revealed in Jesus Christ, and thus, Christians are offered the incommensurable grace to know this face. At the same time, however, Christians have the *responsibility* to live in such a way as to show others the true face of the living God. They are called to radiate to the world the truth that "God is love *(agape)*" (1 Jn 4:8, 16). Since God is love, he is also a Trinity of Persons, whose life consists in their infinite mutual communication in love.

It follows from this that the best way Christians can radiate the truth that God is love is by their own mutual love. "By this all will know that you are my disciples, if you love one another" (Jn 13:35). For this reason, it can be said of Christians that often "to the extent that they neglect their own training in the faith, or teach erroneous doctrine, or are deficient in their religious, moral or social life, they must be said to conceal rather than reveal the authentic face of God and of religion."[90]

---

89. *Gaudium et Spes,* 19.

90. *Ibid.*

Finally, it must be emphasized that the mentioning of these faults of Christians of the past is not only to confess them to Christ the Savior, but also to praise the Lord of history for his merciful love. Christians, in fact, do not believe only in the existence of sin, but also, and above all, in the *forgiveness of sins.* In addition, recalling these faults means accepting our solidarity with those who, in good and bad, have gone before us on the way of truth. It offers to those of the present a powerful reason to convert to the requirements of the Gospel, and it provides a necessary prelude to the request for God's forgiveness that opens the way for mutual reconciliation.

6. Pastoral and Missionary Perspectives

In light of these considerations, it is now possible to ask the question: What are the pastoral aims of the Church's taking responsibility for past faults committed in her name by her sons and daughters, and for which she makes amends? What are its implications for the life of the People of God? And what are the consequences in relation to the Church's missionary effort and her dialogue with various cultures and religions?

6.1. The Pastoral Aims

The following are some of the pastoral reasons for acknowledging the faults of the past.

First, these acts tend toward the *purification of memory,* which—as noted above—is a process aimed at a new evaluation of the past, capable of having a considerable effect on the present, because past sins frequently make their weight felt and remain temptations in the present as well. Above all, if the causes of possible resentment for evils suffered and the negative influences stemming from what was done in the past can be removed as a result of dialogue and the patient search for mutual understanding with those who feel injured by words and deeds of the past, such a removal may help the community of the Church grow in holiness through reconciliation and peace in obedience to the truth.

"Acknowledging the weaknesses of the past," the Pope emphasizes, "is an act of honesty and courage which helps us to strengthen our faith, which alerts us to face today's temptations and challenges, and prepares us to meet them."[91] To that end, it is good that the remembering of faults also includes all possible omissions, even if only some of these are mentioned frequently today. One should not forget the price paid by many Christians for their fidelity to the Gospel and for their service to their neighbor in charity.[92]

A second pastoral aim, closely connected to the first, is the promotion of the continual *reform of the People of God.* "Therefore, if the influence of events or of the times has led to deficiencies in moral conduct, in Church discipline, or even in the way in which doctrine is expressed (which must be carefully distinguished from the deposit of the faith itself), these should be appropriately rectified at the proper moment."[93]

All of the baptized are called to "examine their fidelity to the will of Christ concerning the Church, and as required,

91. *Tertio Millennio Adveniente,* 33.

92. One need only think of the sign of martyrdom: cf. *Tertio Millennio Adveniente,* 37.

93. *Unitatis Redintegratio,* 6. It is the same text which states that "Christ summons the Church, as she goes her pilgrim way, to that continual reform *(ad hanc perennem reformationem)* of which she always has need, insofar as she is a human institution here on earth."

strenuously undertake the work of renewal and reform."[94] The criterion of true reform and of authentic renewal must be fidelity to the will of God regarding his people[95] that presupposes a sincere effort to free oneself from all that leads away from his will, whether we are dealing with present faults or the inheritance from the past.

A further aim can be seen to be the *witness* that the Church gives to the God of mercy and to his liberating and saving truth, from the experience which she has had and continues to have of him in history. There is also the *service* which the Church in this way gives to humanity to help overcome current evils. John Paul II states that "many cardinals and bishops expressed the desire for a serious examination of conscience above all on the part of the Church today. On the threshold of the new millennium Christians need to place themselves humbly before the Lord and examine themselves on the responsibility which they too have for the evils of our day"[96] in order to help overcome them in obedience to the splendor of saving truth.

6.2. The Ecclesial Implications

What are the implications for the life of the Church of an ecclesial request for forgiveness? A number of aspects can be mentioned.

---

94. "*...opus renovationis nec non reformationis...*": *ibid.*, 4.

95. *Ibid.*, 6: "Every renewal of the Church consists essentially in the increase of faithfulness to her vocation."

96. *Tertio Millennio Adveniente,* 36.

It is necessary above all to take into account the different processes of *reception* of acts of ecclesial repentance, because these will vary according to religious, cultural, political, social and personal contexts. In this light, one needs to consider that events or words linked to a contextualized history do not necessarily have a universal significance, and vice versa, that acts conditioned by a determined theological and pastoral perspective have had powerful consequences for the spread of the Gospel (one thinks, for example, of the various historical models of the theology of mission).

Furthermore, there needs to be an evaluation of the relationship between the spiritual benefits and the possible costs of such acts, taking into account also the undue accentuation which the media may give to certain aspects of the Church's statements. One should always remember the Apostle Paul's admonition to welcome, consider, and support the "weak in faith" with prudence and love (cf. Rom 14:1). In particular, attention must be given to the history, the identity, and the current situation of the Eastern Churches and those Churches which exist in continents or countries where the Christian presence is a minority.

It is necessary to specify the *appropriate subject* called to speak about the faults of the past, whether it be local bishops, considered personally or collegially, or the universal Pastor, the Bishop of Rome. In this perspective, it is opportune to take into account—in recognizing past wrongs and the present day subjects who could best assume responsibility for these—the distinction between Magisterium and authority in the Church. Not every act of authority has magisterial value, and so behavior contrary to the Gospel by one or more persons vested with authority does not involve *per se* the magisterial charism, which is assured by the Lord to the Church's bishops, and consequently does not require any magisterial act of reparation.

It is necessary to underscore that *the one addressed* by any request for forgiveness is God and that any human recipients—above all, if these are groups of persons either inside or outside the community of the Church—must be identified with appropriate historical and theological discernment, in order to undertake acts of reparation which are indeed suitable, and also in order to give witness to them of the good will and the love for the truth of the Church's sons and daughters.

This will be accomplished to the extent that there is dialogue and reciprocity between the parties, oriented toward a possible reconciliation connected with the recognition of faults and repentance for them. However, one should not forget that reciprocity—at times impossible because of the religious convictions of the dialogue partner—cannot be considered an indispensable condition, and that the gratuity of love often expresses itself in unilateral initiatives.

Possible gestures of *reparation* must be connected to the recognition of a responsibility which has endured through time, and may therefore assume a symbolic-prophetic character, as well as having value for effective reconciliation (for example, among separated Christians). It is also desirable that in the definition of these acts there be joint research with those who will be addressed, by listening to the legitimate requests which they may present.

On the *pedagogical* level, it is important to avoid perpetuating negative images of the other, as well as causing unwarranted self-recrimination, by emphasizing that, for believers, taking responsibility for past wrongs is a kind of sharing in the mystery of Christ, crucified and risen, who took upon himself the sins of all. Such an interpretation, rooted in Christ's Paschal Mystery, is able in a particular way to produce fruits of liberation, reconciliation and joy for all those who, with living faith, are involved in the request for forgiveness—both the subjects and those addressed.

6.3. The Implications for Dialogue and Mission

On the level of dialogue and mission, the foreseeable implications of the Church's acknowledgment of past faults are varied.

On the level of *the Church's missionary effort,* it is important that these acts do not contribute to a lessening of zeal for evangelization by exacerbating negative aspects. At the same time, it should be noted that such acts can increase the credibility of the Christian message, since they stem from obedience to the truth and tend to produce fruits of reconciliation. In particular, with regard to the precise topics of such acts, those involved in the Church's mission *ad gentes* should take careful account of the local context in proposing these, in light of the capacity of people to receive such acts (thus, for example, aspects of the history of the Church in Europe may well turn out to have little significance for many non-European peoples).

With respect to *ecumenism,* the purpose of ecclesial acts of repentance can be none other than the unity desired by the Lord. Therefore, it is hoped that they will be carried out reciprocally, though at times prophetic gestures may call for a unilateral and absolutely gratuitous initiative.

On the *interreligious* level, it is appropriate to point out that, for believers in Christ, the Church's recognition of past wrongs is consistent with the requirements of fidelity to the Gospel, and therefore constitutes a shining witness of faith in the truth and mercy of God as revealed by Jesus. What must be avoided is that these acts be mistaken as confirmation of possible prejudices against Christianity.

It would also be desirable if these acts of repentance would stimulate the members of other religions to acknowledge the faults of their own past. Just as the history of humanity is full of violence, genocide, violations of human rights and the rights of peoples, exploitation of the weak and glorification of the powerful, so too the history of the various religions is marked by intolerance, superstition, complicity with unjust powers, and the denial of the dignity and freedom of conscience. Christians have been no exception and are aware that all are sinners before God!

In the dialogue with *cultures,* one must, above all, keep in mind the complexity and plurality of the notions of repentance and forgiveness in the minds of those with whom we dialogue. In every case, the Church's taking responsibility for past faults should be explained in the light of the Gospel and of the presentation of the crucified Lord, who is the revelation of mercy and the source of forgiveness, in addition to explaining the nature of ecclesial communion as a unity through time and space.

In the case of a culture that is completely alien to the idea of seeking forgiveness, the theological and spiritual reasons which motivate such an act should be presented in appropriate fashion, beginning with the Christian message and taking into account its critical-prophetic character. Where one may be dealing with a prejudicial indifference to the language of faith, one should take into account the possible double effect of an act of repentance by the Church: on the one hand, negative prejudices or disdainful and hostile attitudes might be confirmed; on the other hand, these acts share in the mysterious attraction exercised by the "crucified God."[97]

One should also take into account the fact that in the current cultural context, above all of the West, the invitation to a purification of memory involves believers and non-believers alike in a common commitment. This common effort is itself already a positive witness of docility to the truth.

Lastly, in relation to *civil society,* consideration must be given to the difference between the Church as a mystery of grace and every human society in time. Emphasis must also be given, however, to the character of exemplarity of the Church's requests for forgiveness, as well as to the consequent stimulus this may offer for undertaking similar steps for purification of memory and reconciliation in other situations where it might be urgent. John Paul II states:

> The request for forgiveness...primarily concerns the life of the Church, her mission of proclaiming salvation, her witness to Christ, her commitment to unity, in a word, the consistency which should distinguish Christian life. But the light and strength of the Gospel, by which the Church lives, also have the

97. This particular strong formulation comes from St. Augustine, *De Trinitate* I, 13, 28: *CCL* 50, 69, 13; *Epist.* 169, 2: *CSEL* 44, 617; *Sermo* 341A, 1: *Misc. Agost.* 314, 22.

capacity, in a certain sense, to overflow as illumination and support for the decisions and actions of civil society, with full respect for their autonomy.... On the threshold of the third millennium, we may rightly hope that political leaders and peoples, especially those involved in tragic conflicts fueled by hatred and the memory of often ancient wounds, will be guided by the spirit of forgiveness and reconciliation exemplified by the Church and will make every effort to resolve their differences through open and honest dialogue.[98]

---

98. John Paul II, *Discourse* to the participants in the International Symposium of study on the Inquisition, sponsored by the Historical-Theological Commission of the Central Committee of the Jubilee, n. 5; October 31, 1998.

Conclusion

At the conclusion of this reflection, it is appropriate to stress yet again that in every form of repentance for the wrongs of the past, and in each specific gesture connected with it, the Church addresses herself in the first place to God and seeks to give glory to him and to his mercy. Precisely in this way she is able to celebrate the dignity of the human person called to the fullness of life in faithful covenant with the living God: "The glory of God is man fully alive; but the life of man is the vision of God."[99]

By such actions, the Church also gives witness to her trust in the power of the truth that makes us free (cf. Jn 8:32). Her "request for pardon must not be understood as an expression of false humility or as a denial of her two thousand-year history, which is certainly rich in merit in the areas of charity, culture and holiness. Instead she responds to a necessary requirement of the truth, which, in addition to the positive aspects, recog-

99. "*Gloria Dei vivens homo: vita autem hominis visio Dei*"*:* St. Irenaeus of Lyons, *Adversus Haereses* IV, 20, 7: *SC* 100/2, 648.

nizes the human limitations and weaknesses of the various generations of Christ's disciples."[100]

Recognition of the truth is a source of reconciliation and peace because, as the Holy Father also states, "Love of the truth, sought with humility, is one of the great values capable of reuniting the men of today through the various cultures."[101] Because of her responsibility to truth, the Church "cannot cross the threshold of the new millennium without encouraging her children to purify themselves, through repentance, of past errors and instances of infidelity, inconsistency and slowness to act. Acknowledging the weaknesses of the past is an act of honesty and courage...."[102] It opens a new tomorrow for everyone.

---

100. John Paul II, *General Audience Discourse* of September 1, 1999; in *L'Osservatore Romano,* Eng. ed., September 8, 1999, 7.

101. *Discourse at the Centre de l'Organisation europeénne pour la recherche nucléaire,* Geneva (June 15, 1982) in *Insegnamenti di Giovanni Paolo II,* V, 2, (Vatican, 1982), 2321.

102. *Tertio Millennio Adveniente,* 33.

Appendix

HOMILY OF THE HOLY FATHER "DAY OF PARDON"

Sunday, March 12, 2000

1. *"We implore you, in Christ's name: be reconciled to God! For our sake God made him who did not know sin to be sin, so that in him we might become the righteousness of God"* (2 Cor 5:20–21).

These are words of St. Paul which the Church rereads every year on Ash Wednesday, at the beginning of Lent. In the Lenten season, the Church desires to be particularly united to Christ, who, moved inwardly by the Holy Spirit, began his messianic mission by going into the wilderness and fasting there for forty days and forty nights (cf. Mk 1:12–13).

At the end of that fast he was tempted by Satan, as we are told briefly by the Evangelist Mark in today's liturgy (cf. 1:13). Matthew and Luke, on the other hand, deal more amply with Christ's struggle in the desert and with his definitive victory over the tempter: "Begone, Satan! For it is written, 'You shall worship the Lord your God and him only shall you serve'" (Mt

4:10). The One speaking in this way is he "who did not know sin" (2 Cor 5:21), Jesus, "the Holy One of God" (Mk 1:24).

2. *"He made him who did not know sin to be sin"* (2 Cor 5:21). A few moments ago, in the second reading, we heard this surprising assertion made by the Apostle. What do these words mean? They seem, and in effect are, a paradox. How could God, who is holiness itself, "make" his Only-begotten Son, sent into the world, "to be sin"? Yet this is exactly what we read in the passage from St. Paul's Second Letter to the Corinthians. We are in the presence of a mystery: a mystery which at first sight is baffling, but is clearly written in divine revelation.

Already in the Old Testament, the Book of Isaiah speaks of it with inspired foresight in the fourth song of the Servant of Yahweh: "We had all gone astray like sheep, each following his own way, but the Lord laid upon him the guilt of us all" (Is 53:6).

Although Christ, the Holy One, was absolutely sinless, he agreed to take our sins upon himself. He agreed in order to redeem us; he agreed to bear our sins to fulfill the mission he had received from the Father, who—as the Evangelist John writes—"so loved the world that he gave his only Son, that whoever believes in him...may have eternal life" (Jn 3:16).

3. Before Christ who, out of love, took our guilt upon himself, we are all invited to make a *profound examination of conscience.* One of the characteristic elements of the Great Jubilee is what I described as the "purification of memory" (Bull *Incarnationis Mysterium,* 11). As the Successor of Peter, I asked that "in this year of mercy the Church, strong in the holiness which she receives from her Lord, should kneel before God and implore forgiveness for the past and present sins of

her sons and daughters" (*Incarnationis Mysterium,* 11). Today, the First Sunday of Lent, seemed to me the right occasion for the Church, gathered spiritually around the Successor of Peter, to implore divine forgiveness for the sins of all believers. *Let us forgive and ask forgiveness!*

This appeal has prompted a thorough and fruitful reflection, which led to the publication several days ago of a document of the International Theological Commission entitled: *Memory and Reconciliation: The Church and the Faults of the Past.* I thank everyone who helped to prepare this text. It is very useful for correctly understanding and carrying out the authentic request for pardon, based on the *objective responsibility* which Christians share as members of the Mystical Body, and which spurs today's faithful to recognize, along with their own sins, the sins of yesterday's Christians, in the light of careful historical and theological discernment.

Indeed, "because of the bond which unites us to one another in the Mystical Body, all of us, though not personally responsible and without encroaching on the judgment of God who alone knows every heart, bear the burden of the errors and faults of those who have gone before us" (*Incarnationis Mysterium,* 11). The recognition of past wrongs serves to *reawaken our consciences to the compromises of the present,* opening the way to conversion for everyone.

4. *Let us forgive and ask forgiveness!* While we praise God who, in his merciful love, has produced in the Church a wonderful harvest of holiness, missionary zeal, total dedication to Christ and neighbor, we cannot fail to recognize *the infidelities to the Gospel committed by some of our brethren,* especially during the second millennium. Let us ask pardon for the divi-

sions which have occurred among Christians, for the violence some have used in the service of the truth and for the distrustful and hostile attitudes sometimes taken toward the followers of other religions.

Let us confess even more *our responsibilities as Christians for the evils of today.* We must ask ourselves what our responsibilities are regarding atheism, religious indifference, secularism, ethical relativism, the violations of the right to life, disregard for the poor in many countries.

We humbly ask forgiveness for the part which each of us has had in these evils by our own actions, thus helping to disfigure the face of the Church.

At the same time, as we confess our sins, *let us forgive the sins committed by others against us.* Countless times in the course of history Christians have suffered hardship, oppression and persecution because of their faith. Just as the victims of such abuses forgave them, so let us forgive as well. The Church today feels and has always felt obliged to *purify her memory* of those sad events from every feeling of rancor or revenge. In this way the Jubilee becomes for everyone a favorable opportunity for a profound conversion to the Gospel. The acceptance of God's forgiveness leads to the commitment to forgive our brothers and sisters and to be reconciled with them.

5. But what does the word "reconciliation" mean to us? To grasp its precise sense and value, we must first recognize the possibility of division, of separation. Yes, man is the only creature on earth who can have a relationship of communion with his Creator, but he is also *the only one who can separate himself from him.* Unfortunately, he has frequently turned away from God.

Fortunately many people, like the prodigal son spoken of in the Gospel of Luke (cf. Lk 15:13), after leaving their father's house and squandering their inheritance, reach the very bottom and realize how much they have lost (cf. Lk 15:13–17). Then they set out to return home: "I will arise and go to my father, and I will say to him, 'Father, I have sinned...'" (Lk 15:18).

God, clearly represented by the father in the parable, welcomes every prodigal child who returns to him. He welcomes him through Christ, in whom the sinner can once again become "righteous" with the righteousness of God. He welcomes him, because for our sake he made his eternal Son to be sin. Yes, only through Christ can we become the righteousness of God (cf. 2 Cor 5:21).

6. *"God so loved the world that he gave his only Son."* Here, in synthesis, is what the mystery of the world's redemption means! We must fully understand the value of the great gift the Father has given us in Jesus. We must keep the eyes of our soul fixed on Christ—the Christ of Gethsemane, Christ scourged, crowned with thorns, carrying the cross and finally crucified. Christ took upon himself the burden of the sins of all people, the burden of our own sins, so that through his saving sacrifice we might be reconciled to God.

Today, Saul of Tarsus who became St. Paul, stands before us as a witness: he had an extraordinary experience of the power of the cross on the way to Damascus. The risen Christ revealed himself to him in all his dazzling power: "'Saul, Saul, why do you persecute me?'... 'Who are you, Lord?'... 'I am Jesus, whom you are persecuting'" (Acts 9:4–5). Today Paul, who had such a powerful experience of the cross of Christ, addresses a fervent prayer to us: *"We beg you not to receive the grace of God in vain."* This grace is offered to us, St. Paul insists, by God himself, who tells us today: *"In an acceptable time I have heard you; on a day of salvation I have helped you"* (2 Cor 6:1–2).

Mary, Mother of forgiveness, help us to accept the grace of forgiveness which the Jubilee generously offers us. Make the Lent of this extraordinary Holy Year an acceptable time, a time of reconciliation, a time of salvation for all believers and for everyone who is searching for God!

The Daughters of St. Paul operate book and media centers at the following addresses. Visit, call or write the one nearest you today, or find us on the World Wide Web, www.pauline.org

California
3908 Sepulveda Blvd., Culver City, CA 90230; 310-397-8676
5945 Balboa Ave., San Diego, CA 92111; 858-565-9181
46 Geary Street, San Francisco, CA 94108; 415-781-5180

Florida
145 S.W. 107th Ave., Miami, FL 33174; 305-559-6715

Hawaii
1143 Bishop Street, Honolulu, HI 96813; 808-521-2731
Neighbor Islands call: 800-259-8463

Illinois
172 North Michigan Ave., Chicago, IL 60601; 312-346-4228

Louisiana
4403 Veterans Memorial Blvd., Metairie, LA 70006; 504-887-7631

Massachusetts
Rte. 1, 885 Providence Hwy., Dedham, MA 02026; 781-326-5385

Missouri
9804 Watson Rd., St. Louis, MO 63126; 314-965-3512

New Jersey
561 U.S. Route 1, Wick Plaza, Edison, NJ 08817; 732-572-1200

New York
150 East 52nd Street, New York, NY 10022; 212-754-1110
78 Fort Place, Staten Island, NY 10301; 718-447-5071

Ohio
2105 Ontario Street, Cleveland, OH 44115; 216-621-9427

Pennsylvania
9171-A Roosevelt Blvd., Philadelphia, PA 19114; 215-676-9494

South Carolina
243 King Street, Charleston, SC 29401; 843-577-0175

Tennessee
4811 Poplar Ave., Memphis, TN 38117; 901-761-2987

Texas
114 Main Plaza, San Antonio, TX 78205; 210-224-8101

Virginia
1025 King Street, Alexandria, VA 22314; 703-549-3806

Canada
3022 Dufferin Street, Toronto, Ontario, Canada M6B 3T5; 416-781-9131
1155 Yonge Street, Toronto, Ontario, Canada M4T 1W2; 416-934-3440

¡También somos su fuente para libros, videos y música en español!